PIANO · VOCAL · GUITAR

The *Best of* RODGERS AND HART

2ND EDITION

ISBN 978-0-7935-2865-3

WILLIAMSON MUSIC®
AN IMAGEM COMPANY™
www.williamsonmusic.com

EXCLUSIVELY DISTRIBUTED BY
HAL•LEONARD®
CORPORATION
7777 W. BLUEMOUND RD. P.O. BOX 13819 MILWAUKEE, WI 53213

Visit Hal Leonard Online at
www.halleonard.com

Contents

BEWITCHED

from PAL JOEY

Words by LORENZ HART
Music by RICHARD RODGERS

BLUE MOON

Music by RICHARD RODGERS
Lyrics by LORENZ HART

THE BLUE ROOM
from THE GIRL FRIEND

Words by LORENZ HART
Music by RICHARD RODGERS

14

DANCING ON THE CEILING

from SIMPLE SIMON
from EVERGREEN

Words by LORENZ HART
Music by RICHARD RODGERS

FALLING IN LOVE WITH LOVE

from THE BOYS FROM SYRACUSE

Words by LORENZ HART
Music by RICHARD RODGERS

28

GLAD TO BE UNHAPPY

from ON YOUR TOES

Words by LORENZ HART
Music by RICHARD RODGERS

Reflectively

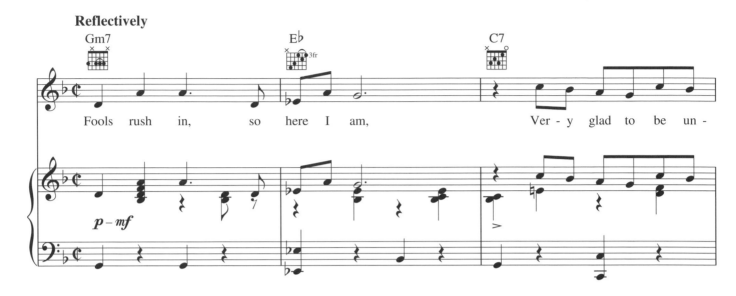

Fools rush in, so here I am, Ver-y glad to be un-

hap-py. _____ I can't win, but here I am, More than glad to be un

hap-py. _____ Un-re-quit-ed love's a bore, And I've got it pret-ty

HAVE YOU MET MISS JONES?

from I'D RATHER BE RIGHT

Words by LORENZ HART
Music by RICHARD RODGERS

HE WAS TOO GOOD TO ME

from SIMPLE SIMON

Words by LORENZ HART
Music by RICHARD RODGERS

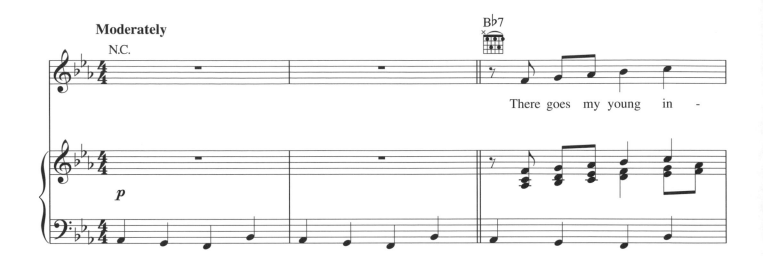

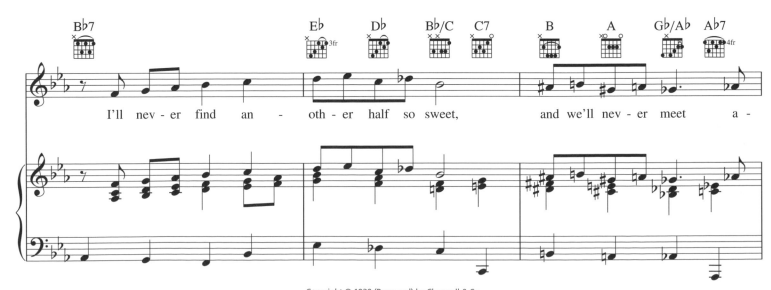

I COULD WRITE A BOOK

from PAL JOEY

Words by LORENZ HART
Music by RICHARD RODGERS

I DIDN'T KNOW WHAT TIME IT WAS

from TOO MANY GIRLS

Words by LORENZ HART
Music by RICHARD RODGERS

I WISH I WERE IN LOVE AGAIN

from BABES IN ARMS

Words by LORENZ HART
Music by RICHARD RODGERS

IT NEVER ENTERED MY MIND

from HIGHER AND HIGHER

Words by LORENZ HART
Music by RICHARD RODGERS

IT'S EASY TO REMEMBER

from the Paramount Picture MISSISSIPPI

Words by LORENZ HART
Music by RICHARD RODGERS

ISN'T IT ROMANTIC?
from the Paramount Picture LOVE ME TONIGHT

Words by LORENZ HART
Music by RICHARD RODGERS

JOHNNY ONE-NOTE

from BABES IN ARMS

Words by LORENZ HART
Music by RICHARD RODGERS

John-ny could on-ly sing one note and the

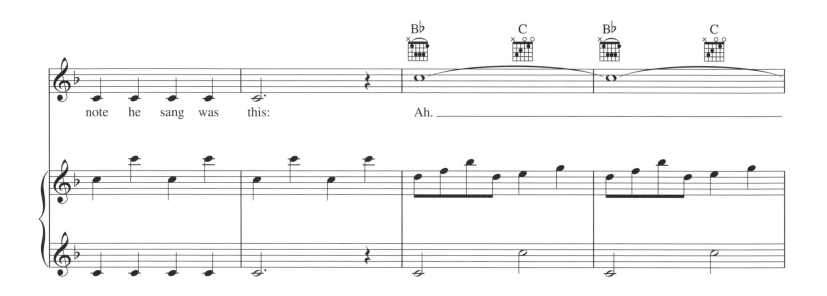

note he sang was this: Ah.

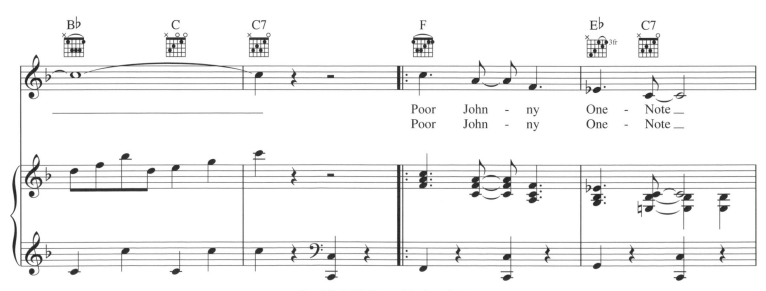

Poor John-ny One-Note ___
Poor John-ny One-Note ___

THE LADY IS A TRAMP

from BABES IN ARMS
from WORDS AND MUSIC

Words by LORENZ HART
Music by RICHARD RODGERS

LITTLE GIRL BLUE

from JUMBO

Words by LORENZ HART
Music by RICHARD RODGERS

Sit there and count your fin - gers, what can you do? Old girl, you're through.

Sit there and count your lit - tle fin - gers, Un -

LOVER

from the Paramount Picture LOVE ME TONIGHT

Words by LORENZ HART
Music by RICHARD RODGERS

8vb

MANHATTAN
from the Broadway Musical THE GARRICK GAIETIES

Words by LORENZ HART
Music by RICHARD RODGERS

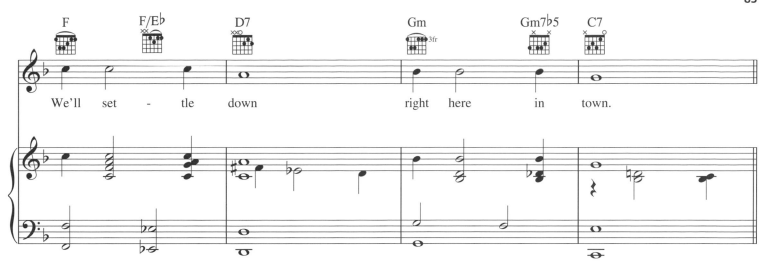

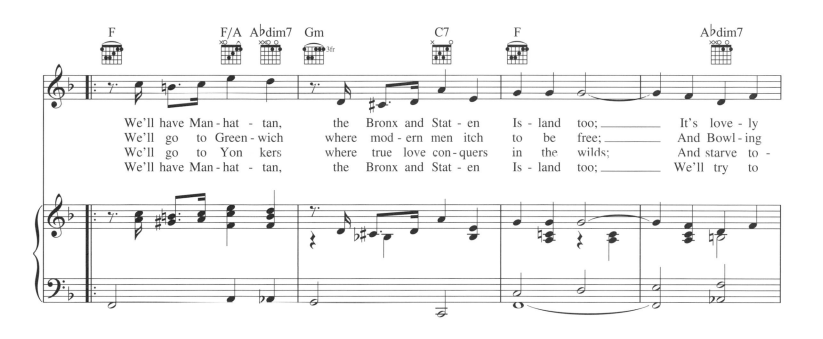

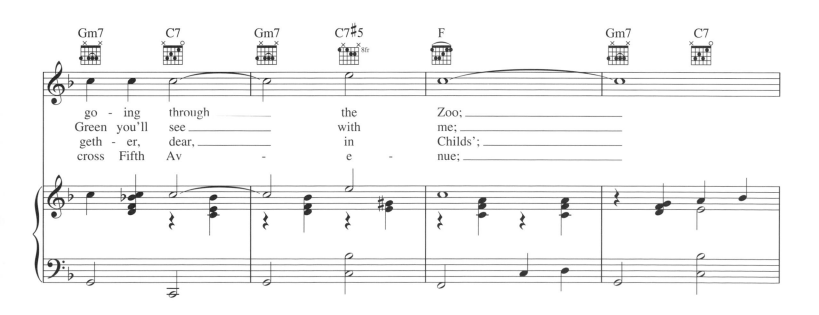

84

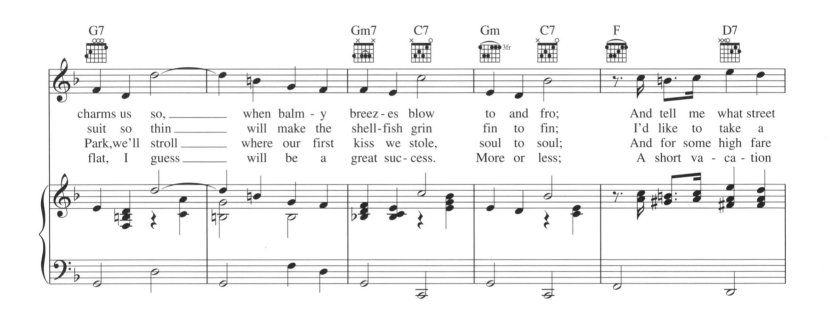

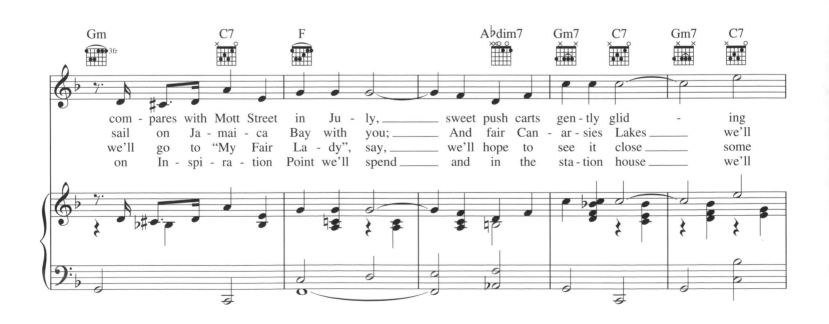

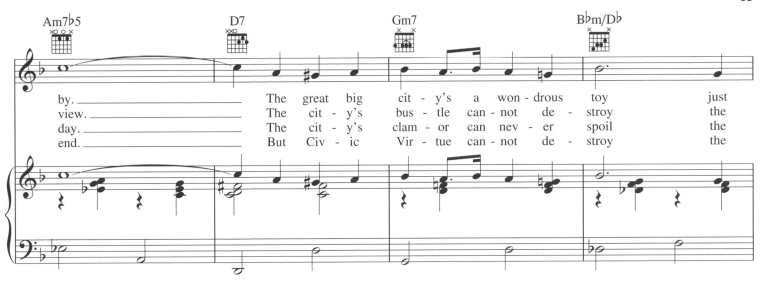

by. _____ The great big cit - y's a won - drous toy just
view. _____ The cit - y's bus - tle can - not de - stroy the
day. _____ The cit - y's clam - or can nev - er spoil the
end. _____ But Civ - ic Vir - tue can - not de - stroy the

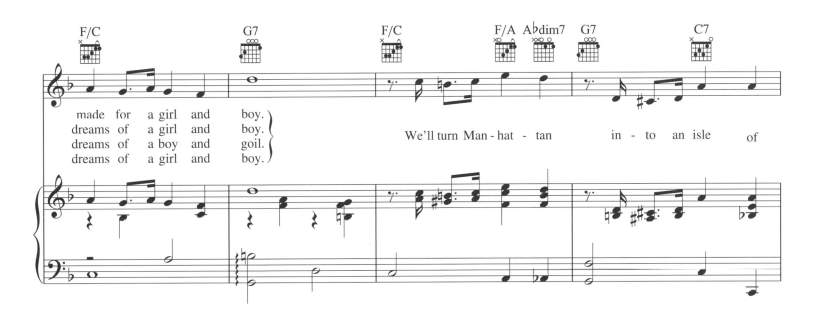

made for a girl and boy.
dreams of a girl and boy.
dreams of a boy and goil.
dreams of a girl and boy.

We'll turn Man - hat - tan in - to an isle of

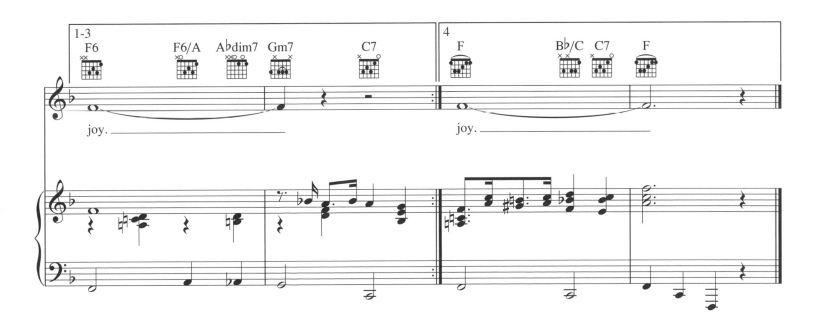

joy. _____ joy. _____

MIMI
from the Paramount Picture LOVE ME TONIGHT

Words by LORENZ HART
Music by RICHARD RODGERS

89

THE MOST BEAUTIFUL GIRL IN THE WORLD

from JUMBO

Words by LORENZ HART
Music by RICHARD RODGERS

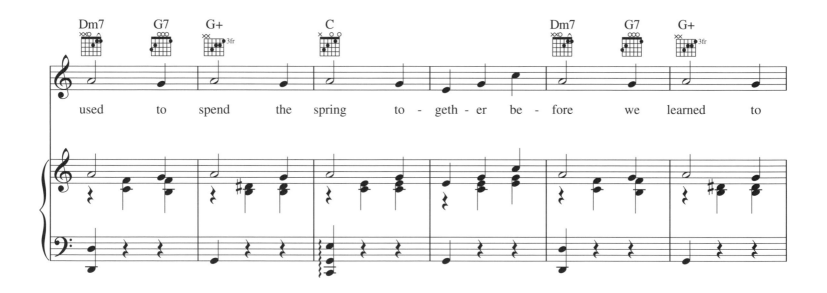

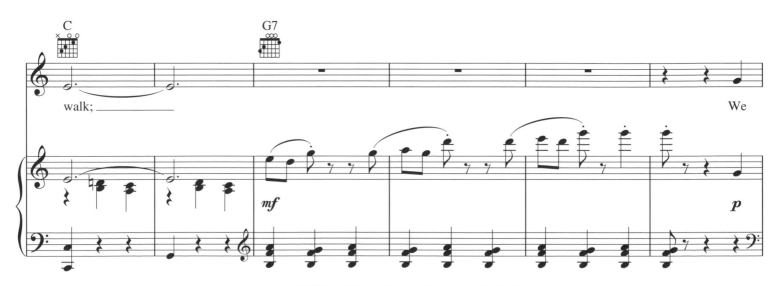

sea - son has a rea - son, And there's spring - time in my

heart. _____

The most

beau - ti - ful girl in the world _____ Picks my ties out, eats my

MOUNTAIN GREENERY

from the Broadway Musical THE GARRICK GAIETIES

Words by LORENZ HART
Music by RICHARD RODGERS

MY FUNNY VALENTINE
from BABES IN ARMS

Words by LORENZ HART
Music by RICHARD RODGERS

MY HEART STOOD STILL

from A CONNECTICUT YANKEE

Words by LORENZ HART
Music by RICHARD RODGERS

109

110

MY ROMANCE

from JUMBO

Words by LORENZ HART
Music by RICHARD RODGERS

114

NOBODY'S HEART
from BY JUPITER

Words by LORENZ HART
Music by RICHARD RODGERS

long to me, No ____ arms feel strong to me,

I ad - mire the moon, As a moon,

Just a moon, No - bod - y's heart be - longs to me to -

day.

day. ____

8vb

TEN CENTS A DANCE

from SIMPLE SIMON

Words by LORENZ HART
Music by RICHARD RODGERS

122

SPRING IS HERE

from I MARRIED AN ANGEL

Music by RICHARD RODGERS
Lyrics by LORENZ HART

Once there was a thing called spring, when the world was writ-ing vers-es like yours and mine. All the lads and girls would sing, When we sat at lit-tle ta-bles and drank May wine. Now A-pril, May and June

127

THERE'S A SMALL HOTEL

from ON YOUR TOES

Words by LORENZ HART
Music by RICHARD RODGERS

THIS CAN'T BE LOVE
from THE BOYS FROM SYRACUSE

Words by LORENZ HART
Music by RICHARD RODGERS

THOU SWELL
from A CONNECTICUT YANKEE
from WORDS AND MUSIC

Words by LORENZ HART
Music by RICHARD RODGERS

135

WAIT TILL YOU SEE HER

from BY JUPITER

Words by LORENZ HART
Music by RICHARD RODGERS

My friends who knew me, nev-er would know me.

They'd look right through me, a-bove and be-

low me and ask, "Who's that man?"

YOU TOOK ADVANTAGE OF ME

from PRESENT ARMS

Words by LORENZ HART
Music by RICHARD RODGERS

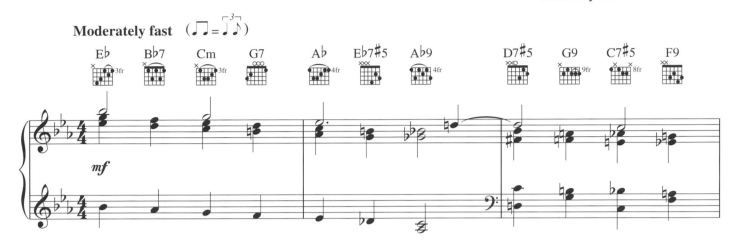

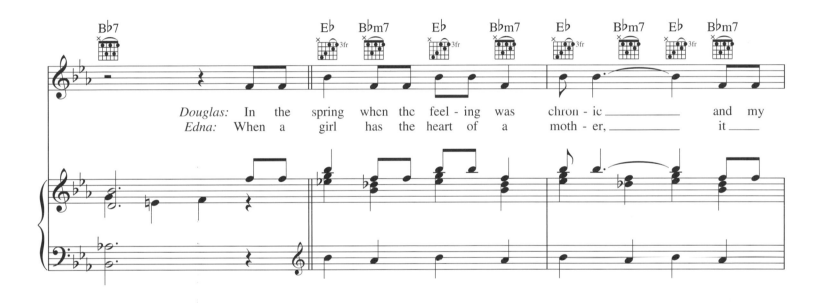

Douglas: In the spring when the feel-ing was chron-ic _____ and my
Edna: When a girl has the heart of a moth-er, _____ it

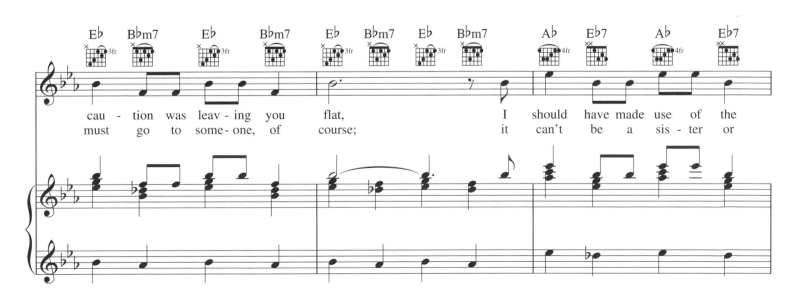

cau-tion was leav-ing you flat, I should have made use of the
must go to some-one, of course; it can't be a sis-ter or

146

WHERE OR WHEN

from BABES IN ARMS

Words by LORENZ HART
Music by RICHARD RODGERS

150

WITH A SONG IN MY HEART
from SPRING IS HERE

Words by LORENZ HART
Music by RICHARD RODGERS

YOU ARE TOO BEAUTIFUL

from HALLELUJAH, I'M A BUM

Words by LORENZ HART
Music by RICHARD RODGERS

159